RECIPES

*Traditional Fare
from around
the county*

*with illustrations by
Gordon Home*

SALMON

Index

Cover pictures; *front:* Haworth Church and Parsonage   *back:* Cottages at Runswick Bay
Title page: Whitby Harbour

Printed and Published by J. Salmon Ltd., Sevenoaks, England © Copyright

Yorkshire Teacakes

A teatime favourite, toasted and served warm and spread with plenty of butter.

1 lb strong white flour	**4 oz currants**
1 level teaspoon salt	**2 oz chopped mixed peel**
2 oz butter	**$^1/_2$ oz fresh yeast**
1 oz caster sugar	**$^1/_2$ pint tepid milk**

Milk to glaze

Grease and flour baking sheets. Cream the yeast with a little of the tepid milk. Sift the flour and salt together into a bowl and rub in the butter to resemble breadcrumbs. Stir in the sugar, currants and peel. Make a well in the centre of the mixture, add the creamed yeast and then stir in sufficient of the tepid milk to make a soft but not sticky dough. Turn out on to a floured surface and knead until the dough is elastic. Return to the lightly greased or floured bowl, cover with a clean cloth and leave in a warm place to rise until doubled in size. When risen, cut into 8 equal pieces and work lightly into rounds about 6 inches in diameter. Put on to the baking sheet, brush with milk, cover and leave to prove until risen. Meanwhile, set oven to 400° F or Mark 6. Bake for about 20 minutes until brown. Transfer to a wire rack to cool.

Yorkshire Yule Cake

*A cake which was traditionally made to offer to callers at the Festive Season
with cheese and a glass of wine or beer; it improves with keeping.*

**1 lb flour   1 teaspoon salt   3 oz lard
4 oz butter $^{1}/_{2}$ oz fresh yeast   6 - 7 fl. oz tepid water
6 oz soft brown sugar $^{1}/_{4}$ teaspoon mixed spice $^{1}/_{4}$ teaspoon grated nutmeg
12 oz currants   1 egg, beaten**

Grease and line a 7 inch cake tin. Cut the lining to stand up 1 to 2 inches above the
edge of the tin to make a collar. Sift the flour and salt together into a bowl and rub
in the lard and butter to resemble breadcrumbs. Cream the yeast with a little of the
tepid water and add to the mixture. Blend in the sugar with sufficient of the
remaining water to beat to a smooth dough. Transfer to a floured surface and knead
thoroughly. Return to the lightly greased or floured bowl, cover with a clean cloth
and leave in a warm place to rise until doubled in size. When risen, knock back the
dough, work in the spices, currants and beaten egg and knead again for 2 to 3
minutes. Put into the tin, cover and leave to prove until risen. Meanwhile, set oven
to 400° F or Mark 6. Bake for 50 to 60 minutes or until golden brown and a
skewer inserted comes out clean. Leave to cool in the tin then turn out on a wire rack.

Ovington Fruit Cake

*A light, lemon flavoured fruit cake that originates from beside the River Tees
in the north of the county.*

8 oz flour   **³/₄ teaspoon baking powder**   **8 oz ground rice**
7 oz butter, softened   **8 oz caster sugar**   **Grated rind of 2 lemons**
12 oz currants   **3 eggs, beaten**   **Milk to mix**

Set oven to 350° F or Mark 4. Grease and line a 9 to 10 inch cake tin. Sift the
flour, baking powder and ground rice together into a bowl. Rub in the butter until
the mixture resembles breadcrumbs. Add the sugar, lemon rind and currants and
stir together. Mix in the 3 eggs and sufficient milk to produce a dropping consistency. Spoon into the tin and bake for about 1½ to 2 hours or until a skewer
inserted comes out clean. Leave to cool in the tin and turn out on to a wire rack.

Startforth Gingerbread

North of England gingerbreads date from the 19th century when the introduction of bicarbonate of soda for aeration produced the thick light cakes of today, unlike the biscuit types of previous centuries.

4 oz butter	½ teaspoon bicarbonate of soda
2 oz brown sugar	1 teaspoon mixed spice
8 oz black treacle	Pinch ground ginger
8 oz flour	2 eggs, beaten
	2 fl. oz sour milk

Set oven to 375° F or Mark 5. Grease and line a 1 lb loaf tin. Melt together the butter, sugar and treacle in a pan over a low heat. Sift together the flour and bicarbonate of soda, mixed spice and ginger and stir the flour mixture into the treacle mixture. Add the beaten eggs and sour milk and mix thoroughly. Pour into the tin and bake for 1½ to 2 hours or until a skewer inserted comes out clean. Turn out on to a wire rack and cut into slices when cold.

Fat Rascals

Teatime in Yorkshire cannot be considered complete without Fat Rascals on the table. They are a cross between a sweet scone and a rock cake.

8 oz self-raising flour	**2 oz currants**
¹/₂ teaspoon salt	**1 oz sultanas**
4 oz lard	**1 egg, beaten**
3 oz caster sugar	**Milk to mix**

Set oven to 425° F or Mark 7. Grease baking sheets. Sift the flour and salt together into a bowl and rub in the lard until the mixture resembles breadcrumbs. Stir in the sugar, currants and sultanas and mix to a soft dough with the beaten egg and a little milk if necessary. Transfer to a lightly floured surface, roll or press out to a good ¹/₂ inch thick and cut out into 2¹/₂ inch rounds with a cutter. Place apart on the baking sheet and bake for about 10 to 15 minutes until golden. Transfer to a wire rack to cool. Eat fresh with butter. Makes about 12 scones.

Yorkshire Curd Tart

A fresh tasting tart using curds sweetened with dried fruit and spiced with nutmeg.

8 oz rich shortcrust pastry	**2 oz currants**
8 oz fresh curds (approx)	**2 eggs, beaten**
4 oz caster sugar	**Grated nutmeg for sprinkling**

Set oven to 350° F or Mark 4. Grease an 8 inch flan dish. Roll out the pastry on a lightly floured surface and line the dish. Put the curds, sugar and currants into a bowl and mix together with the beaten eggs. Spoon the mixture into the dish, smooth out and sprinkle with grated nutmeg. Bake for 25 to 30 minutes until set and golden. Leave in the dish to get cold and then cut into segments. To make curds, take 2 pints of sour milk or 2 pints fresh milk soured with 2 dessertspoons lemon juice or vinegar. Boil the milk until it curdles and forms solids, leave to cool and then strain through muslin. Rinse the curds in cold water and drain. This should yield about 8 oz of curds.

Ginger Snaps

Deliciously irresistible, gingery, crispy biscuits.

8 oz flour	**3 oz caster sugar**
1½ teaspoons baking powder	**4 oz lard**
1 dessertspoon ground ginger	**4 oz golden syrup**

½ a small beaten egg

Set oven to 350° F or Mark 4. Grease baking sheets. Sift the flour, baking powder and ginger into a bowl and stir in the sugar. Melt the lard and syrup together in a pan over a low heat and mix into the dry ingredients, with the egg, to produce a stiff paste. Take teaspoonsful of the mixture, roll into walnut-size balls with floured hands and set out, well apart, on the baking sheet. Bake for about 15 minutes until golden brown. Leave the biscuits to cool on the sheet before transferring to a wire rack. Makes about 30 biscuits.

Yorkshire Mint Pasty

A sweet pasty containing dried fruit and mixed peel and flavoured with fresh mint.

1 lb puff pastry or ¾ lb sweet shortcrust pastry
2 oz currants   2 oz raisins   1 oz chopped candied peel   1½ oz soft brown sugar
Pinch grated nutmeg   1 tablespoon chopped fresh mint   1½ oz butter, softened
Milk for glazing   Caster sugar for dusting

Set oven to 425° F or Mark 6. Grease baking sheets. Roll out the pastry on a floured surface to ¼ inch thick and cut into 8 rounds. In a bowl, mix the currants, raisins, candied peel, sugar, nutmeg and mint and bind all together with the butter. Divide the mixture evenly over one half of each pastry round. Fold over the pastry, damp the edge and seal well. Brush with milk, sprinkle with caster sugar and bake for about 30 minutes until golden brown. Transfer to a wire rack to cool.

Oat Cakes

These biscuits make a perfect accompaniment to Wensleydale cheese.

8 oz fine oatmeal   **Pinch bicarbonate of soda**
½ level teaspoon salt   **1 oz butter, softened**
Cold water to mix

Set oven to 300° F or Mark 2. Grease a baking sheet. Put the oatmeal, salt and bicarbonate of soda into a bowl. Rub in the butter and add just enough cold water to mix to a firm dough. Knead lightly on a surface dusted with oatmeal until the dough is smooth. Roll out thinly and cut into round biscuits with a plain cutter. Place on the baking sheet and bake for about 1 hour until crisp. Transfer to a wire rack to cool. Serve cold with butter and cheese.

Harrogate Sponge

A fat-less sponge filled with jam and/or whipped cream or with butter icing; best eaten fresh.

4 eggs   4 oz caster sugar   2 tablespoons boiling water   4 oz flour
³/₄ teaspoon baking powder
Jam, butter icing or whipped cream for filling   Icing sugar for dusting

Set oven to 375° F or Mark 5. Grease and bottom line two 8 inch sandwich tins. Beat together the eggs and sugar in a bowl set over a pan of hot water until the mixture becomes thick and creamy; remove from the heat. Add the 2 tablespoons of boiling water and continue beating for 5 minutes. Fold in half the sifted flour and baking powder and then stir in the remainder. Put half of the mixture into each tin, spread out and bake for 20 minutes or until a skewer inserted comes out clean. Transfer to a wire rack to cool. When cold, sandwich the cake with jam, whipped cream or butter icing. Dust the top with sifted icing sugar. To make butter icing, cream 3 oz softened butter with 6 oz sifted icing sugar, add a few drops of vanilla flavouring and mix in a little warm water to make a spreading consistency.

Leeds Parkin

Parkin is a form of gingerbread which originated in Yorkshire and always includes oatmeal in the ingredients.

8 oz flour	½ teaspoon bicarbonate of soda
8 oz butter, softened	2 lb medium oatmeal
8 oz caster sugar	2 lb golden syrup
4 teaspoons ground ginger	2½ fl. oz milk

Set oven to 350° F or Mark 4. Grease and flour an 8 inch square 2 inch deep cake tin or equivalent. Sift the flour into a bowl and rub in the butter until the mixture resembles breadcrumbs. Add the sugar, ground ginger, bicarbonate of soda and oatmeal and mix well together. Put the syrup and milk into a pan and mix together over a gentle heat. Add gradually to the dry ingredients, mixing well to a fairly stiff consistency. Put into the tin, smooth out and bake for 45 to 60 minutes until golden. Leave in the tin to cool. When cold, mark out into small squares with a fork pushed in to make perforations, turn out and break apart.

Shrimp Paste

No High Tea is complete without shrimp paste. Prawns can be used if preferred.

12 oz whole shrimps	**Good pinch cayenne pepper**
8 oz cod or haddock fillets	**Good pinch ground mace**
2 anchovy fillets	**Pinch of salt**
1 teaspoon anchovy essence	**5 oz butter, softened**

3 - 4 oz clarified butter for sealing

If using fresh shrimps, boil for 2 to 3 minutes and allow to cool. Shell the shrimps, cut up the flesh roughly and set aside. Wash the shells, put in a pan, just cover with water and boil for 20 minutes. Strain off the liquid and use to simmer the cod or haddock fillets until cooked. Remove the fish from the pan and boil the liquid hard to reduce it to about 2 tablespoons. Put the fish, the reduced liquid and all the other ingredients, except the shrimps, into a food processor and blend to a smooth paste. Transfer to a bowl and work in the chopped shrimps. Pack the mixture into small pots and cover and seal with clarified butter. Store in a cool place. To make clarified butter, put the butter into a pan, bring to the boil and remove from the heat. The clear butter liquid will come to the top. Pour off very gently, as required, leaving the sediment in the bottom of the pan.

Yorkshire Kipper Paste

Kipper paste is another High Tea favourite. In Yorkshire, only hard-boiled eggs and butter are added to the fish. Use unsalted butter or the paste may be too salty.

2 large kippers   **10 oz unsalted butter, softened**
2 hard-boiled eggs   **3 - 4 oz clarified butter for sealing**

Stand the kippers, head down, in a large jug of boiling water for about 10 minutes or lay in a casserole dish and cover with water. Drain the fish well and remove the flesh from the skin and bones. Roughly chop the kipper flesh and the hard-boiled eggs, put into a food processor with the butter and blend to a smooth paste. Pack the mixture into small pots and cover and seal with clarified butter. Store in a cool place. To make clarified butter see Shrimp Paste recipe.

Yorkshire Scones

*Scones are the epitome of English afternoon tea. The essential of a Yorkshire Scone is
that it is cut into a round not less than 1 inch thick before baking.*

1 lb self-raising flour	**4 oz sugar**
1 teaspoon salt	**2 eggs**
4 oz butter	**5 fl. oz milk**
1 beaten egg for glazing	

Set oven to 425° F or Mark 6. Grease and flour baking sheets. Sift the flour and salt
into a bowl and rub in the butter until the mixture resembles breadcrumbs. Stir in
the sugar. Make a well in the centre, drop in the eggs and gradually work in the
milk, bringing in the flour from the sides until the dough is smooth and elastic.
Transfer to a floured surface and roll or press out lightly to 1 inch thick. Cut out
rounds with a 2 inch plain cutter, brush with beaten egg and place on the baking
sheet. Bake for about 10 minutes until golden. Transfer to a wire rack to cool.

Yorkshire Treacle Tart

*Unlike traditional treacle tart, this version has dried fruit and grated apple
added to the syrup mixture.*

12 oz sweet shortcrust pastry
FILLING

6 oz mixed dried fruit	**Grated rind and juice $1/2$ lemon**
2 oz grated apple	**3 oz golden syrup**

$1^1/_2$ oz fresh brown breadcrumbs

Set oven to 425° F or Mark 7. Butter an 8 inch pie plate. Roll out the pastry on a lightly floured surface and use half to line the pie plate. Mix all the ingredients together in a bowl and spread the mixture over the pastry base. Cover with the remaining pastry and damp and seal the edge. Bake for 10 to 15 minutes then reduce oven to 350ºF or Mark 4 and bake for about a further 30 minutes until golden. Leave on the plate to cool.

Ilkley Cake

A spicy fruit cake made with dripping instead of the more usual lard or butter.

1 lb flour	4 oz dripping
$\frac{1}{2}$ teaspoon salt	12 oz soft brown sugar
$3\frac{1}{2}$ teaspoons baking powder	8 oz currants
1 teaspoon mixed spice	4 oz raisins
1 teaspoon grated nutmeg	2 oz chopped mixed peel

Cold water to mix

Set oven to 350° F or Mark 4. Grease and line an 8 to 9 inch cake tin. Sift the flour, salt, baking powder and spices into a bowl and rub in the fat until the mixture resembles breadcrumbs. Stir in the sugar, currants, raisins and candied peel and mix to a dropping consistency with just sufficient cold water. Put into the tin and bake for about 2 hours or until a skewer inserted comes out clean. Leave in the tin to cool and turn out on to a wire rack.

York Biscuits

A thin, sweet biscuit which can be eaten on its own or with cheese.

6 oz butter, softened   **6 oz caster sugar**   **1 lb flour**
1½ teaspoons baking powder   **5 fl. oz milk**

Set oven to 325° F or Mark 3. Grease baking sheets. Beat together the butter and sugar in a bowl until light and fluffy. Sift in the flour and baking powder and fold in. Mix to a stiff dough with sufficient of the milk. Transfer to a lightly floured surface and roll out to no more than ⅛ inch thick. Cut into 2 inch rounds with a cutter. Arrange the biscuits on the baking sheet and bake for about 30 minutes until golden. Makes about 36 biscuits.

Sticky Parkin

Sticky Parkin is best kept in a tin for about a week before eating to allow it to become really moist; hence the name 'sticky'.

8 oz flour	**6 oz black treacle**
2 level teaspoons baking powder	**4 oz hard margarine**
2 level teaspoons ground ginger	**6 oz soft brown sugar**
1 level teaspoon ground cinnamon	**1 egg, beaten**
8 oz medium oatmeal	**¼ pint milk**

Set oven to 350° F or Mark 4. Grease and line a 9 inch square cake tin or equivalent. Sieve the flour, baking powder, ginger and cinnamon into a bowl and stir in the oatmeal. Put the treacle, margarine and sugar into a pan over a low heat and stir occasionally until the margarine has just melted. Make a well in the centre of the dry ingredients and gradually stir in the treacle mixture and then the egg and milk. Beat well until smooth. Pour into the tin and bake for about 1 hour until golden. Cool slightly in the tin and turn out on to a wire rack. Store in an airtight tin. Serve on its own or spread with butter.

Yorkshire Rabbit

This dish is quick to prepare and is ideal for the traditional High Tea;
it is also known as Buck Rabbit.

8 oz Cheddar cheese, grated	**$^1\!/_2$ teaspoon made English mustard**
1 oz butter	**Salt and pepper**
2$^1\!/_2$ fl. oz milk or ale	**4 poached eggs**
Worcestershire Sauce	**4 slices toast**

Pre-heat the grill. Put the grated cheese in a pan with the butter, milk or ale, a few drops of Worcestershire sauce and the mustard with salt and pepper to taste. Stir over a low heat until the mixture is the consistency of thick cream and keep warm. Meanwhile, poach the eggs and toast the bread. Pour the cheese mixture over the toasts and brown under the grill. Top with the poached eggs and serve immediately. Serves 4.

Bedale Plum Cake

A very rich fruit cake with a light crumbly texture; a good keeper.

1 lb butter, softened	**2 teaspoons mixed spice**
1 lb caster sugar	**8 oz raisins**
9 eggs	**8 oz currants**
18 oz flour	**8 oz sultanas**
1½ teaspoons baking powder	**4 oz chopped mixed peel**

Grated rind and juice of 1 lemon

Set oven to 350° F or Mark 4. Grease and line a 9 to 10 inch cake tin. Cream the butter and sugar together in a bowl until light and fluffy. Beat the eggs in a bowl set over a pan of hot water until creamy and whisk in the creamed butter/sugar mixture. Sift together the flour, baking powder and mixed spice and fold into the mixture in the bowl. Stir in the dried fruit, mixed peel and lemon rind and juice and mix to a soft consistency. Put into the tin, make a depression in the centre and bake for about 2 hours or until a skewer inserted comes out clean. Leave in the tin to cool and turn out on to a wire rack.

Curd Tarts

The mixture to fill these little tarts adds cream and whipped egg whites to the fresh curds and is flavoured with lemon.

8 oz sweet shortcrust pastry	**2 eggs, separated**
8 oz fresh curds (approx)	**2 oz caster sugar**
2½ fl. oz cream	**Vanilla essence**

Juice and grated rind of 1 lemon

Set oven to 350° F or Mark 4. Grease about 16 patty tins. Roll out the pastry on a lightly floured surface. Cut out circles with a cutter and line the patty tins. Rub the curds through a coarse sieve into a bowl and beat in the cream, egg yolks, sugar, a few drops of vanilla essence and the lemon juice and rind. Beat the egg whites stiffly and carefully fold into the mixture. Put a spoonful of mixture into each patty case and bake for 25 to 30 minutes until set and golden. Turn out on to a wire rack to cool. To make curds see Yorkshire Curd Tart.

Oven Bottom Cake

Originally this dough cake was made with surplus dough left over from breadmaking.
It is eaten hot with butter and/or jam.

1½ lb strong white flour	**2½ teaspoons granulated sugar**
2 teaspoons salt	**15 fl. oz tepid water**
½ oz fresh yeast	**4 oz lard, diced**

Grease and flour a baking sheet. Cream the yeast with the sugar and a little of the tepid water and leave to stand until frothy. Sift the flour and salt into a bowl and pour in the yeast mixture and the remaining water and mix to a smooth dough. Turn out on to a floured surface and knead until smooth and elastic. Return to the lightly greased or floured bowl, cover with a clean cloth and leave in a warm place to rise until doubled in size. When risen, knock back the dough and knead lightly for 2 to 3 minutes. Next, push the diced lard into the dough and knead, using the knuckle. The dough will be lumpy. Press out into a round and place on the baking sheet. Cover and leave to prove until risen. Meanwhile, set oven to 425° F or Mark 7. Bake for 10 minutes then reduce the heat to 375° F or Mark 5 and bake for about another 35 minutes until golden brown. Cool on a wire rack.

Rhubarb Gingerbread

This unusual gingerbread incorporates a layer of rhubarb and crystallised ginger through the centre.

2 oz butter	3 level teaspoons ground ginger
2 oz caster sugar	1 egg, beaten
1½ oz black treacle	Milk to mix
4 oz flour	6 oz rhubarb, cut into small pieces
½ teaspoon bicarbonate of soda	6 oz crystallised ginger, roughly chopped

Set oven to 350° F or Mark 4. Grease and fully line an 8 inch square shallow cake tin. Melt the butter, sugar and treacle together in a pan over a low heat; remove from the heat. Sift together the flour, bicarbonate of soda and 1 level teaspoon of the ground ginger and stir into the mixture in the pan. Stir in the beaten egg and enough milk to give a soft consistency. Spoon half the mixture into the tin, top evenly with the rhubarb pieces and crystallised ginger and sprinkle over the remaining 2 level teaspoons ground ginger. Spoon over the remaining gingerbread mixture and spread out. Bake for about 1 to 1½ hours or until a skewer inserted comes out clean. Cut into squares when cold.

Cable Cakes

These fruit buns contain mincemeat instead of the more usual dried fruit.

2 oz caster sugar	1 lb flour
4 oz lard	1 oz baking powder
1 lb mincemeat	2 eggs
5 fl.oz milk (approx)	

Set oven to 450° F or Mark 8. Grease patty tins. Cream the sugar and lard together in a bowl until light and fluffy and stir in the mincemeat. Sift together the flour and baking powder, stir into the mincemeat mixture and mix well together. Put the eggs and milk into a bowl and beat together. Stir sufficient of the egg/milk mixture gradually into the dry mixture to make a stiff dough. Spoon the mixture into the patty tins and bake for about 15 minutes until golden. Turn out on a wire rack to cool.

Harrier Cake

A plain date and walnut cake which is best eaten within a day or two.

¹/₂ lb flour	4 oz caster sugar
¹/₂ oz bicarbonate of soda	¹/₂ lb chopped dates
³/₄ teaspoon baking powder	2 oz chopped walnuts
1 teaspoon mixed spice	1 oz black treacle or golden syrup
4 oz butter, softened	1 egg, beaten

¹/₂ pint milk (approx)

Set oven to 350° F or Mark 4. Grease and line a 6 to 7 inch cake tin. Sift the flour, bicarbonate of soda, baking powder and spice together into a bowl. Rub in the butter until the mixture resembles breadcrumbs. Add the sugar and fold in the chopped dates and walnuts. Mix in the treacle or syrup and the beaten egg with the milk to a dropping consistency. Spoon into the tin and bake for 1¹/₂ to 2 hours or until a skewer inserted comes out clean. Leave in the tin to cool before turning out on a wire rack.

Drop Scones

A simple treat and an ideal standby to make for the unexpected visitor as they are quick to prepare from normal store-cupboard ingredients.

8 oz self-raising flour   **¹/₂ teaspoon salt**   **1 level tablespoon caster sugar**
1 large egg, beaten   **¹/₂ pint milk**

Put the flour, salt and sugar into a bowl. Make a well in the centre and gradually stir in the beaten egg and milk to make a smooth, thick batter. Drop tablespoons of the mixture on to a hot, lightly greased griddle or heavy based frying pan. Keep the griddle at a steady, moderate heat and after 2 to 3 minutes, when bubbles show on the surface of the scones, turn over and cook for 2 minutes more. Put the finished scones, as they are cooked, in a warm, folded tea towel; this will keep them warm and by keeping in the steam will prevent them from drying out. Serve warm with butter and jam or honey.

Honey Cake

A rich, honey and lemon flavoured cake with a spicy, peel topping.

6 oz butter, softened   4 oz caster sugar   4 oz honey
Grated rind of 1 lemon   6 eggs $^3/_4$ lb self-raising flour
TOPPING
1 oz ground cinnamon   1 oz honey   4 oz chopped mixed peel

Set oven to 325° F or Mark 3. Grease and line a 7 inch cake tin. Cream together the butter, sugar and honey in a bowl until light and fluffy. Add the grated lemon rind and beat in the eggs, one at a time. Finally, fold in the sifted flour. For the topping, mix together the cinnamon, honey and mixed peel and spread over the base of the tin. Carefully spoon in the cake mixture and bake for 1 to 1½ hours or until a skewer inserted comes out clean. Leave to cool in the tin before turning out with the spicy mixture on top.

York Buns

Little round buns filled with currants and mixed peel.

1 lb flour	6 oz currants
1 oz baking powder	2 oz chopped mixed peel
Pinch of salt	2 eggs, beaten
6 oz butter, softened	$^1/_2$ pint milk (approx)
6 oz caster sugar	Beaten egg or milk for glazing

Set oven to 425° F or Mark 7. Grease baking sheets. Sift the flour, baking powder and salt into a bowl and rub in the butter until the mixture resembles breadcrumbs. Mix in the sugar, currants, mixed peel and beaten eggs with sufficient milk to produce a fairly stiff consistency. Shape into small rounds with floured hands, brush with beaten egg or milk and place on the baking sheet. Bake for about 15 to 20 minutes until golden. Transfer to a wire rack to cool.

Yorkshire Parkin

This is another variation of parkin in which beer is incorporated with black treacle in the mixture.

¹/₂ lb flour	4 oz medium oatmeal
1 teaspoon bicarbonate of soda	2 teaspoons ground ginger
3 oz butter, softened	1 egg, beaten
3 oz lard	1 lb black treacle
4 oz fine oatmeal	¹/₂ pt beer

Set oven to 350° F or Mark 4. Grease and flour an 8 inch square shallow cake tin or equivalent. Sift the flour and bicarbonate of soda into a bowl and rub in the butter and lard until the mixture resembles breadcrumbs. Add all the oatmeal and the ground ginger and mix together with the beaten egg to a fairly stiff consistency. Put the treacle and beer into a pan and warm together over a gentle heat. Add gradually to the oatmeal mixture and mix well to a soft, dropping consistency. Spoon into the tin and bake for 45 to 60 minutes until golden. Leave in the tin to cool and then cut into squares.

Yorkshire Orange Jelly

Jellies are always popular at teatime and create a party atmosphere.

Rind of 2 oranges	**1¼ pint water**
Rind of 2 lemons	**5 fl oz orange juice**
½ lb caster sugar	**5 fl oz lemon juice**
2 cloves	**2 oz gelatine**
2 egg whites	**5 fl. oz sherry**

Put the thinly cut peel, the sugar, cloves, egg whites, water and orange and lemon juice into a pan and bring slowly to the boil. Remove from the heat and strain through a jelly bag. Dissolve the gelatine in a little water and whisk into the juice mixture. Return to the pan and simmer gently for 10 minutes. Stir in the sherry and then leave to cool. When cool, pour into a wetted mould and leave to set. When required to serve, dip the mould in hot water and turn out. Alternatively, put to set in individual sundae glasses.

Sly Cakes

A succulent fruit-filled pastry slice which can be made with dates or dried figs as preferred.

12 oz rich shortcrust pastry
FILLING

6 oz dates or dried figs, chopped	**2 oz dark soft brown sugar**
2 oz currants	**Grated rind of $\frac{1}{2}$ a lemon**
2 oz raisins	**6 tablespoons water**
2 oz chopped walnuts	**Caster sugar for dusting**

First prepare the filling. Put all the ingredients, except the caster sugar, into a pan and heat gently, stirring occasionally until the mixture is soft and the water is absorbed. Set aside to cool. Set oven to 375° F or Mark 5. Grease a 9 x 4 inch or equivalent shallow tin. Divide the pastry in half, roll out on a lightly floured surface and use one half to line the tin. Spread the filling evenly over the pastry. Damp the edges and cover with the other half of pastry. Seal the edges well. Bake for about 30 minutes until golden. Sprinkle with caster sugar and leave to cool in the tin. When cold, cut into squares.

Yorkshire Cheesecakes

These small cheesecakes, somewhat similar to Bakewell Pudding, are traditionally baked in Ripon in the first week in August to commemorate St. Wilfrid, the town's patron saint.

8 oz sweet shortcrust pastry	**2 oz ground almonds**
¹/₂ pt milk	**1 oz caster sugar**
1 oz fresh white breadcrumbs	**Grated rind of 1 lemon**
4 oz butter	**3 eggs**

Set oven to 350° F or Mark 4. Grease about 16 patty tins. Roll out the pastry on a lightly floured surface, cut out circles with a cutter and line the patty tins. Put the milk into a pan, bring to the boil and stir in the breadcrumbs. Leave to stand for about 10 minutes. Then add the butter, ground almonds, sugar and lemon rind to the milk mixture and beat in the eggs, one at a time. Spoon sufficient of the mixture into each patty case and bake for 20 to 25 minutes until set. Turn out on to a wire rack to cool.

Wakefield Gingerbread

A gingerbread which contains mixed peel and is combined with golden syrup and brandy.

11 oz self-raising flour	**2 teaspoons ground ginger**
5 oz butter, softened	**1½ oz chopped mixed peel**
5 oz caster sugar	**4 oz golden syrup**
1 dessertspoon brandy	

Set oven to 350° F or Mark 4. Grease and line an 8 inch square shallow cake tin or equivalent. Sift the flour into a bowl and rub in the butter until the mixture resembles breadcrumbs. Add the sugar, ground ginger and mixed peel and stir together. Warm the syrup with the brandy in a pan over a low heat and then add to the mixture in the bowl and work in well to a soft consistency. Spoon into the tin and bake for 1½ to 2 hours or until a skewer inserted comes out clean. Transfer to a wire rack and cut into squares when cold.

Batley Cake

*A round cake made on a baking sheet, not in a tin and with
a layer of jam through the middle.*

12 oz flour	6 oz caster sugar
3$\frac{1}{2}$ teaspoons baking powder	1 egg, beaten
$\frac{1}{2}$ teaspoon salt	Milk to mix
6 oz butter, softened	2 - 3 dessertspoons jam, as preferred

Beaten egg to glaze

Set oven to 350° F or Mark 4. Grease and flour a baking sheet. Sift the flour, baking powder and salt into a bowl and rub in the butter until the mixture resembles breadcrumbs. Mix in the sugar, add the beaten egg and mix to a stiff consistency with only a very little milk, if necessary. Divide the mixture in two and roll out two rounds about $\frac{1}{2}$ inch thick on a lightly floured surface. If the jam is stiff, warm slightly in a bowl over hot water to facilitate spreading. Spread one round with the jam, cover with the other and pinch the edges together. Brush the top with beaten egg, place on the baking sheet and bake for 30 to 35 minutes until golden and a skewer inserted comes out clean. Transfer to a wire rack to cool.

METRIC CONVERSIONS

The weights, measures and oven temperatures used in the preceding recipes can be easily converted to their metric equivalents. The conversions listed below are only approximate, having been rounded up or down as may be appropriate.

Weights

Avoirdupois	Metric
1 oz.	just under 30 grams
4 oz. (¼ lb.)	app. 115 grams
8 oz. (½ lb.)	app. 230 grams
1 lb.	454 grams

Liquid Measures

Imperial	Metric
1 tablespoon (liquid only)	20 millilitres
1 fl. oz.	app. 30 millilitres
1 gill (¼ pt.)	app. 145 millilitres
½ pt.	app. 285 millilitres
1 pt.	app. 570 millilitres
1 qt.	app. 1.140 litres

Oven Temperatures

	°Fahrenheit	Gas Mark	°Celsius
Slow	300	2	150
	325	3	170
Moderate	350	4	180
	375	5	190
	400	6	200
Hot	425	7	220
	450	8	230
	475	9	240

Flour as specified in these recipes refers to plain flour unless otherwise described.